COMPOSER
SHOWCASE
HAL LEONARD
STUDENT PIANO LIBRARY

TWO PIANOS, EIGHT HANDS – INTERMEDIATE LEVEL

Jambalaya

A Portrait of Old New Orleans

ENSEMBLE FOR TWO PIANOS, EIGHT HANDS

ARRANGED BY EUGÉNIE ROCHEROLLE

Commissioned by the Musical Arts Society of New Orleans

T0087809

HAL•LEONARD®
CORPORATION
7777 W. BLUEMOUND RD. P.O. BOX 13819 MILWAUKEE, WI 53213

Visit Hal Leonard Online at
www.halleonard.com

✣

This piece premiered a month before Hurricane Katrina struck.
I would like to dedicate it to the memory of the old city the way I always knew her,
and to those who will never again have the chance to know her.

—*Eugénie Rocherolle*

✣

Jambalaya
A Portrait of Old New Orleans

Piano I

By Eugénie R. Rocherolle

Allegro moderato (♩ = 72)

5

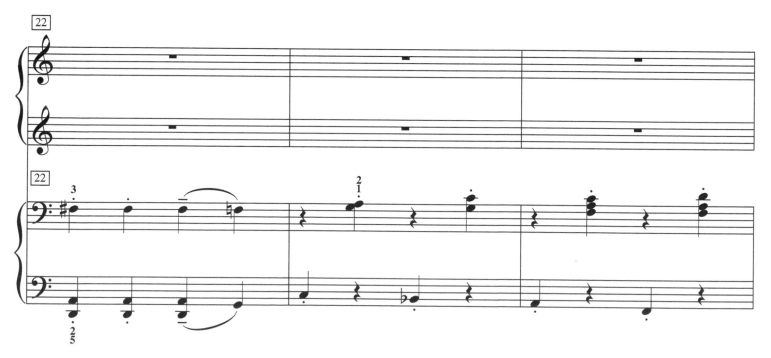

Più mosso (♩♩ = ♩ ♪)

9

10

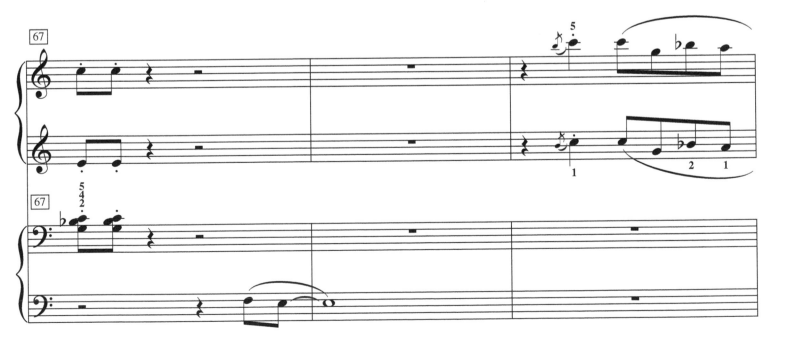

TWO PIANOS, EIGHT HANDS – INTERMEDIATE LEVEL

Jambalaya

A Portrait of Old New Orleans

ENSEMBLE FOR TWO PIANOS, EIGHT HANDS

BY EUGÉNIE ROCHEROLLE

Commissioned by the Musical Arts Society of New Orleans

HAL•LEONARD®
CORPORATION

7777 W. BLUEMOUND RD. P.O. BOX 13819 MILWAUKEE, WI 53213

HL00296654

❦

This piece premiered a month before Hurricane Katrina struck.
I would like to dedicate it to the memory of the old city the way I always knew her,
and to those who will never again have the chance to know her.

—Eugénie Rocherolle

❦

Jambalaya
A Portrait of Old New Orleans

Piano II

By Eugénie R. Rocherolle

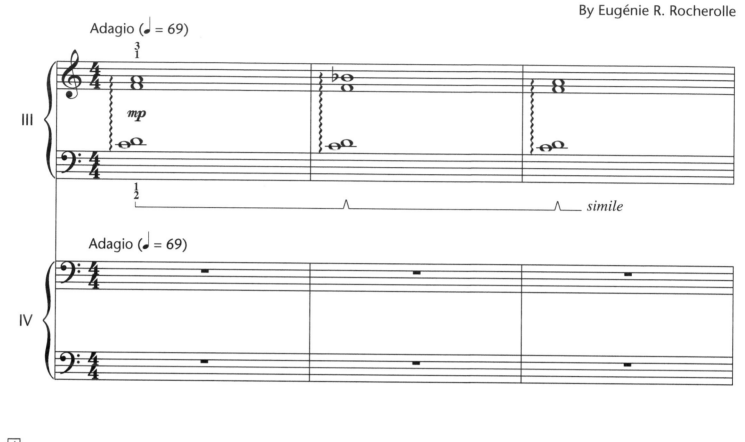

Allegro moderato (♩ = 72)

Allegro moderato (♩ = 72)

9

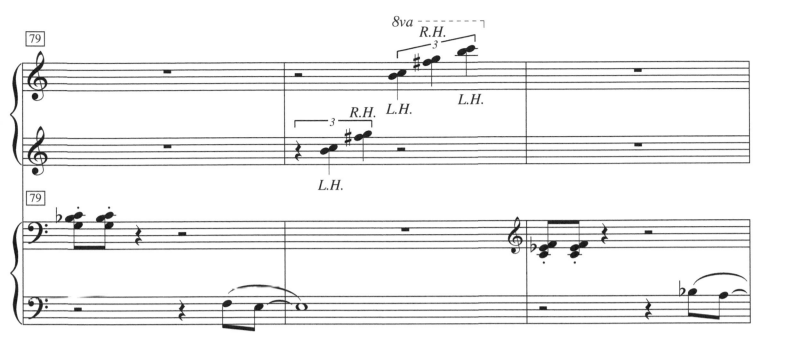

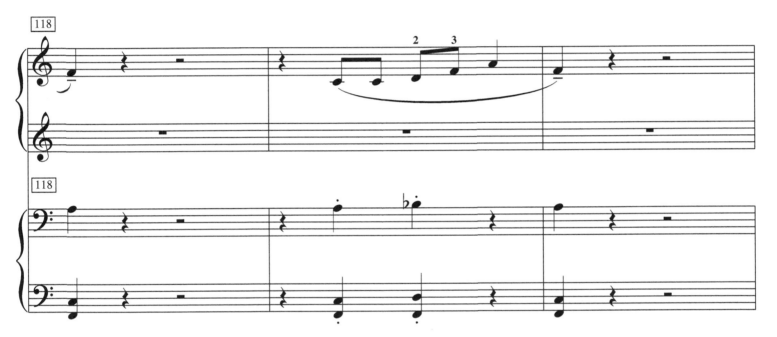

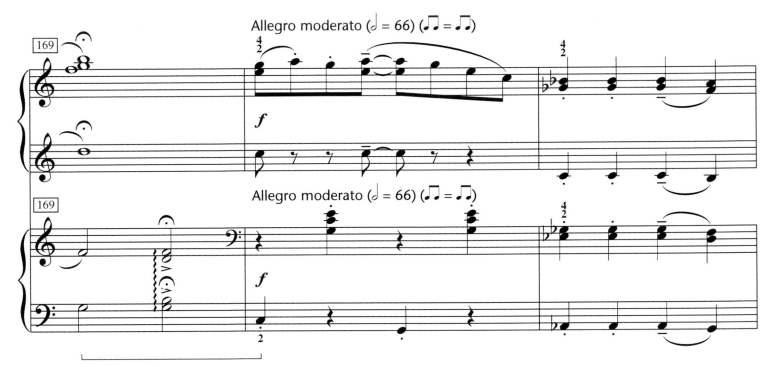

Allegro moderato (♩ = 66) (♪♪ = ♪♪)

*optional

(6'48")

24

dim. poco a poco

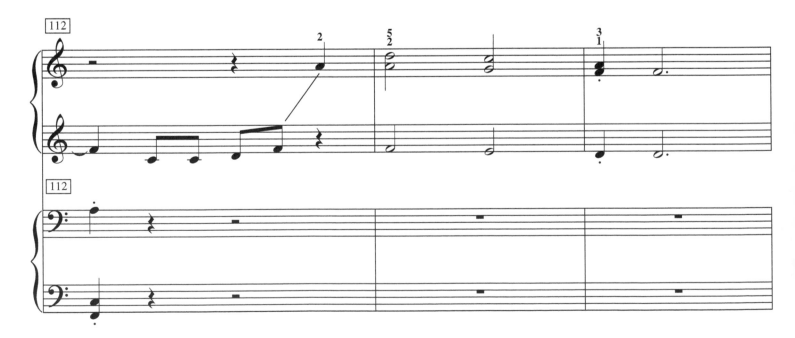

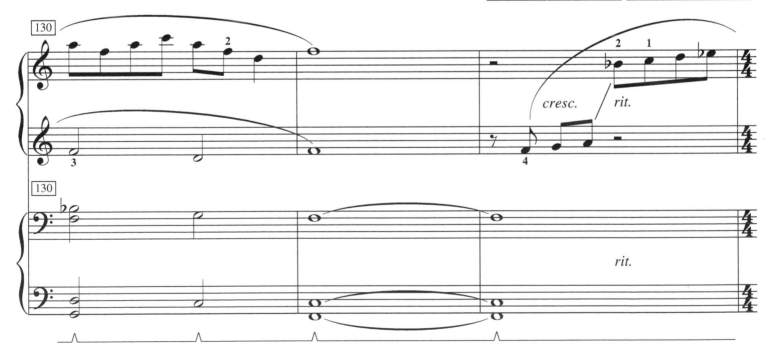

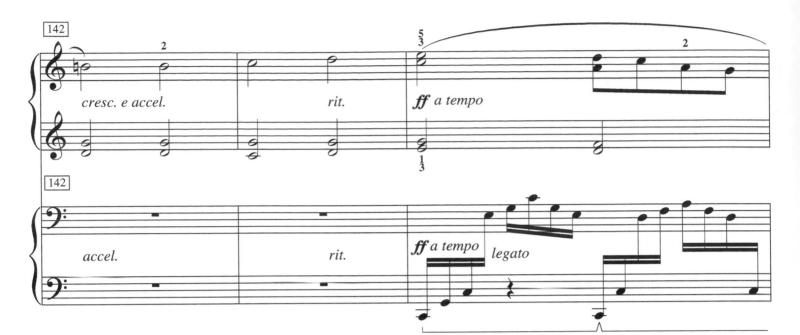

*optional

(6'48")